VEGETARIAN SPROUT

Scrumptious Meatless Barbecue Grilling Recipe Cookbook

BY: Diana Welkins

Although the majority of grilling recipes concentrate on meat, there are several mouthwatering vegetarian recipes to create on the grill. Grilling is all about having a good time and taking pleasure in your friends and families company. All of these tasty recipes will be sure to make an impression as well as bring everyone together over some flavorful and delectable vegetarian grilling recipes. Tofu and sturdy vegetables, such as peppers, mushrooms and eggplant, cook up rather quickly on the grill. The grill delivers vegetables can satisfy vegetarians and die hard meat enthusiasts alike. Regardless of whether you're undertaking some summer time entertaining or simply up for a whole new grilling experience, incorporate some of these vegetarian grilling recipes to your line-up.

What kinds of vegetarian grilling recipes can I expect to get out of this book?

Whenever you mention vegetarians and grilling, quite often tofu dogs or even packaged veggie burgers get introduced into the conversation. However the truth is, there are plenty of yummy (as well as unpackaged) quality recipes that provide vegetarians a significant desire to dust off the barbecue this season.

Take pleasure in an amazing vegetarian cookout with smoky grilled vegetables. We have included meat alternatives, such as veggie burgers nourishing burgers created from beans and grains, vegan pizza, vegan chicken, along with seitan and tofu are additional scrumptious grilling choices.

Grilling tools you will to create a successful vegetarian barbecue grilling experience.

- Gas or charcoal grill

- Grill rack or grill topper

- Silicone basting brush

- Vegetable oil for coating grill rack or grill topper

- Paper towels or clean cotton towel

- Skewers (bamboo or stainless steel)

- Long-handled metal tongs and spatula

Table of Contents

Chapter 4

Chapter 6

Numerous vegetarians delight in enjoying their food on the grill. There is certainly no reason why you cannot enjoy some terrific vegetarian meals which are nourishing and amazingly delicious. When you make a few simple preparations, you will have the ability to create some amazing vegetable meals. You will also discover a considerable amount of grilling recipes for vegetarians and if you follow directions and maintain some effortless suggestions, there is absolutely no reason you cannot get it right. Allow your creativity run and utilize the fresh summer produce to create a spread to savor. With summer months around the corner we will soon be coming into the season for barbecue foods. There are numerous tasty recipes for meat-based barbecue food but many individuals get stuck for ideas when it comes to vegetarian barbecue. Here are some suggestions that will make an excellent addition to any barbecue or a delicious vegetarian choice for friends and family.

Implement the following tips for outstanding results each time you grill.

1. **Pre-heat Properly**

Light the grill, and oil the grate or grill topper with a paper or cloth towel dipped in vegetable oil before cooking. A charcoal grill needs approximately 40 minutes to achieve the preferred temperature, a gasoline grill requires 20 minutes.

2. **Sizing up Your Vegetables**

Ensure the vegetables are sliced the exact same size so that they cook at the same rate. Place ingredients that require longest to cook on the grill first, combine quicker-cooking items after.

3. **Be Safe and Consistent**

Be conscious the fire bears hot spots; shift the vegetables around as soon as they begin to brown. However don't begin moving until items have had the opportunity to sear——usually 3 minutes. This will make for attractive grill marks as well as keeps food from adhering to the grate.

4. Recommended Grilling Tool

 A stainless-steel vegetable grill topper is the most effective investment a vegetarian griller can make. With a vegetable grill topper, the dimensions of vegetables doesn't become a restrictive factor therefore you don't have to be concerned with slices slipping through the grate and into the hot coals.

Tips On How to Take Your Grill's Temperature

Absolutely no thermostat required. Just simply hold your palm 4 inches above the grate and count until your hand starts to feel hot. The following, the times and their associated temperatures:

2-3 seconds = high temperature

4-5 seconds = medium-high temperature

6-8 seconds = medium temperature

9-10 seconds = medium-low temperature

If temperature is too high for your recipe, decrease the temperature on a gasoline grill or shift some coals off to the side in a charcoal grill.

Chapter 1

Grilled Tofu Skewers with Sirach

Prep Time: 15 Minutes

Cook Time: 10 Minutes

Ready In: 1 Hour 25 Minutes

Servings: 2

<u>INGREDIENTS</u>

1 (8 ounce) container extra firm tofu,

Drained and sliced into large chunks

1 zucchini, cut into large chunks

1 red bell pepper, cut into large chunks

10 large mushrooms

2 tablespoons Sirach chili garlic sauce

1/4 cup soy sauce

2 tablespoons sesame oil

1/4 cup diced onion

1 jalapeno pepper, diced

Ground black pepper to taste

<u>INSTRUCTIONS</u>

1. Position tofu, zucchini, red bell pepper, and mushrooms in a bowl. Blend Sirach sauce, soy sauce, sesame oil, onion, jalapeno, and pepper in

a compact bowl, and add over tofu and vegetables. Toss slightly to coat. Cover up, and then allow to marinate a minimum of 1 hour in the fridge.

2. Preheat an outside grill for medium-high heat, and slightly oil the grate.

3. Thread tofu and veggies onto skewers. Grill each skewer 10 minutes, or to wanted doneness. Apply any leftover marinade as a dipping sauce.

Nutrition Facts

Serving Size 453 g

Amount Per Serving

Calories 283   Calories from Fat 172

	% Daily Value*
Total Fat 19.1g	**29%**
Saturated Fat 3.0g	**15%**
Cholesterol 0mg	**0%**
Sodium 1830mg	**76%**
Potassium 1022mg	**29%**
Total Carbohydrates 16.8g	**6%**
Dietary Fiber 5.3g	**21%**
Sugars 8.2g	
Protein 16.9g	

Vitamin A 42%	•	Vitamin C 167%
Calcium 26%	•	Iron 36%

Nutrition Grade A

* Based on a 2000 calorie diet

Nutritional Analysis

Good points

- No cholesterol
- High in iron
- High in manganese
- High in niacin
- High in phosphorus
- High in potassium
- High in riboflavin
- High in selenium
- High in vitamin A
- Very high in vitamin B6
- Very high in vitamin C

Bad points

- Very high in sodium

Marinated Vegetable Medley

Prep Time: 15 Minutes

Cook Time: 15 Minutes

Ready In: 1 Hour

Servings: 8

INGREDIENTS

1/2 cup thickly sliced zucchini

1/2 cup sliced red bell pepper

1/2 cup sliced yellow bell pepper

1/2 cup sliced yellow squash

1/2 cup sliced red onion

16 large fresh button mushrooms

16 cherry tomatoes

1/2 cup olive oil

1/2 cup soy sauce

1/2 cup lemon juice

1/2 clove garlic, crushed

INSTRUCTIONS

1. Position the zucchini, red bell pepper, yellow bell pepper, squash, red onion, mushrooms, and tomatoes in a sizable bowl.

2. In a compact bowl, combine olive-oil, soy sauce, lemon juice, and garlic. Add over the vegetables. Cover up bowl, and marinate in the fridge for half an hour.

3. Preheat grill for moderate heat.

4. Lightly oil grate. Take out vegetables from marinade, and position on preheated Barbecue grill. Grill for 12 to 15 minutes, or until tender.

Nutrition Facts

Serving Size 363 g

Amount Per Serving

Calories 182   Calories from Fat 121

% Daily Value*

Total Fat 13.4g	**21%**
Saturated Fat 2.0g	**10%**
Cholesterol 0mg	**0%**
Sodium 918mg	**38%**
Potassium 837mg	**24%**
Total Carbohydrates 14.3g	**5%**
Dietary Fiber 4.1g	**16%**
Sugars 8.8g	
Protein 5.0g	

Vitamin A 49%	•	Vitamin C 97%
Calcium 3%	•	Iron 13%

Nutrition Grade A

* Based on a 2000 calorie diet

Nutritional Analysis

Good points

- No cholesterol
- High in potassium
- Very high in vitamin A
- Very high in vitamin B6
- Very high in vitamin C

Bad points

- Very high in sodium
- High in sugar

Grilled Fresh Basil Pizza

Prep Time: 45 Minutes

Cook Time: 15 Minutes

Ready In: 3 Hours

Servings: 6

INGREDIENTS

1 (.25 ounce) package active dry yeast

1 cup warm water

1 pinch white sugar

2 teaspoons kosher salt

1 tablespoon olive oil

3 1/3 cups all-purpose flour

2 cloves garlic, minced

1 tablespoon chopped fresh basil

1/2 cup olive oil

1 teaspoon minced garlic

1/4 cup tomato sauce

1 cup chopped tomatoes

1/4 cup sliced black olives

1/4 cup roasted red peppers

2 cups shredded mozzarella cheese

4 tablespoons chopped fresh basil

INSTRUCTIONS

1. In a simple bowl, dissolve yeast in Luke warm water, and combine sugar. Proof for 10 minutes, or until frothy. Add the salt, olive-oil, and flour until dough pulls from the edges of the bowl. Shift onto a lightly floured surface area. Knead until smooth out, for 8 minutes. Position dough in a nicely oiled bowl, and cover up with a moist cloth. Put aside to rise until doubled, approximately 1 hour. Punch down, and knead in garlic and basil. Set aside rise for 1 additional hour, or until doubled again.

2. Preheat grill for high heat. Heat olive-oil with garlic for 30 seconds in the microwave oven. Put aside. Punch down dough, and separate in half. Shape each half into an oblong form 3/8 to 1/2 inch thick.

3. Brush grill grate with garlic flavored olive-oil. Very carefully position one piece of dough on heated grill. The dough will start to puff almost instantly. Once the lower crust has lightly browned, shift the dough over utilizing two spatulas. Working quickly, brush oil over crust, then brush with 2 tablespoons tomato sauce. Prepare 1/2 cup chopped tomatoes, 1/8 cup sliced black olives, and 1/8 cup roasted red peppers over crust. Spread with 1 cup cheese and 2 tablespoons basil. Close up the lid, and cook until the cheese melts. Remove from grill, and put aside to cool down for a couple of minutes then serve.

Nutrition Facts

Serving Size 227 g

Amount Per Serving

Calories 546   Calories from Fat 245

                                          % Daily Value*

Total Fat 27.3g	**42%**
Saturated Fat 6.9g	**35%**
Trans Fat 0.0g	
Cholesterol 20mg	**7%**
Sodium 1127mg	**47%**
Potassium 229mg	**7%**
Total Carbohydrates 57.9g	**19%**
Dietary Fiber 3.0g	**12%**
Sugars 1.9g	
Protein 19.0g	

Vitamin A 18%   •   Vitamin C 31%

Calcium 30%   •   Iron 22%

Nutrition Grade B-

* Based on a 2000 calorie diet

Nutritional Analysis

Good points

- Low in cholesterol
- Low in sugar

Eggplant and Halloumi Sandwich

Prep Time: 10 minutes

Cook Time: 15 minutes

Total Time: 25 minutes

Servings: 4

INGREDIENTS

Oil

Salt and pepper

1 medium eggplant, sliced 1/4 inch thick

8 slices bread

8 ounces halloumi, sliced 1/4 inch thick

2 roasted red peppers, cut into 4 slices

2 cups salad greens

2 large beefsteak tomatoes, sliced 1/4 inch thick

4 tablespoons basil pesto

1/2 lemon, juice

INSTRUCTIONS

1. Slightly brush the eggplant and bread with oil and season the eggplant with salt and pepper.

2. Grill the eggplant over moderate high heat until tender, about 2-4 minutes per side.

3. Lightly grill the bread and halloumi on each side then splash the halloumi with the lemon juice.

4. Put together the sandwiches and enjoy!

Nutrition Facts

Serving Size 263 g

Amount Per Serving

Calories 103   Calories from Fat 10

% Daily Value*

Total Fat 1.1g	**2%**
Cholesterol 0mg	**0%**
Sodium 216mg	**9%**
Potassium 565mg	**16%**
Total Carbohydrates 21.7g	**7%**
Dietary Fiber 6.0g	**24%**
Sugars 8.2g	
Protein 3.7g	

Vitamin A 39%	Vitamin C 130%
Calcium 5%	Iron 8%

Nutrition Grade A

* Based on a 2000 calorie diet

Nutritional Analysis

Good points

- Low in saturated fat
- No cholesterol
- Very high in dietary fiber
- High in manganese
- High in niacin
- High in potassium
- High in thiamin
- Very high in vitamin A
- High in vitamin B6
- Very high in vitamin C

Bad points

- High in sugar

Grilled Portobello Mushrooms & Just Peachy Burgers

Prep Time: 15 Minutes

Cook Time: 50 Minutes

Ready In: 1 Hour 5 Minutes

Servings: 6

INGREDIENTS

6 Portobello mushrooms

6 peaches

6 sweet potatoes

6 burger buns of your choice

100 g fresh pea sprouts

5 small roman tomatoes, sliced

5 small spring onions, sliced

Fresh thyme

Olive oil

Salt & pepper

Marinade INGREDIENTS

4 tbsp. olive oil

2 fresh rosemary sprigs

1 tbsp. fresh thyme

2 garlic cloves

1/2 lemon

Salt & pepper

Guacamole INGREDIENTS

4 avocados

5 small Roma tomatoes

1 garlic clove

1/4 cup parsley

1/2 lemon

1 tbsp. olive oil

INSTRUCTIONS

1. Thoroughly clean the Portobello mushrooms by thoroughly eliminating dirt from the caps with a cooking towel or cloth; you may use some water if necessary. Pat dry. Slice the peaches in halves and take out the pits.

2. Preparing the sweet potato fries: Preheat the oven to 350°F. Slice the sweet potatoes in 1-inch thick, 5-inch long pieces. Place them on a parchment-covered baking sheet. Drizzle olive-oil, salt and thyme over them and place in the oven. The fries require around 30 minutes before they are ready, however you need to stir after 15 minutes.

3. Producing the marinade: Pour olive-oil in a compact bowl. Insert one chopped rosemary sprig, chopped thyme, mashed garlic, freshly squeezed lemon juice and salt and pepper to taste. Stir around. Make use of the other rosemary sprig to brush the mushrooms and peaches with the marinade. Once the grill is ready, grill the Portobello and peaches for about 3 to 4 minutes on both sides, while you use the rosemary stick to brush the marinade over them an additional time.

4. Creating the guacamole: Slice avocados, tomatoes and parsley roughly. Place them to a small bowl with mashed garlic. Squeeze lemon juice over it, and mash everything with a fork. It's alright if it remains a bit chunky.

5. Assembling the burger: Cut the buns in halves. Allow them to get some color on the grill. When finished, put a big dollop of guacamole on the lower bun, and add pea sprouts, tomatoes, spring onion, one Portobello

mushroom and two peach halves. Place the top of the bun, and put in a stick to hold everything together. Enjoy!

Nutrition Facts

Serving Size 329 g

Amount Per Serving

Calories 431	Calories from Fat 344

% Daily Value*

Total Fat 38.3g	**59%**
Saturated Fat 7.2g	**36%**
Trans Fat 0.0g	
Cholesterol 0mg	**0%**
Sodium 14mg	**1%**
Potassium 1051mg	**30%**
Total Carbohydrates 25.1g	**8%**
Dietary Fiber 11.8g	**47%**
Sugars 11.0g	
Protein 4.4g	

Vitamin A 28%	•	Vitamin C 58%
Calcium 5%	•	Iron 11%

Nutrition Grade B

* Based on a 2000 calorie diet

Nutritional Analysis

Good points

- No cholesterol
- Very low in sodium
- High in dietary fiber
- High in vitamin C

Chapter 2

Auvergne & Burgher Salad

Prep Time: 10 Minutes

Cook Time: 10 Minutes

Ready In: 20 Minutes

Servings: 4

INGREDIENTS

175g burgher wheat

2 tbsp. sundried tomato paste

4 baby aborigines, each sliced lengthways into 3

1 red pepper, sliced lengthways into 1cm pieces

2 tsp olive oil

Handful basil leaves

INSTRUCTIONS

Prepare burgher following package INSTRUCTIONS. Tip into a sizable bowl and stir through the tomato paste. Season.

Heat up a Barbecue or grill pan to high. Drizzle the aborigines and red pepper with the oil and grill for 5 mines on both sides until slightly charred.

Mix the aborigines and red pepper into the burgher mix, then season and stir through the basil.

Nutrition Facts

Serving Size 32 g

Amount Per Serving

Calories 29 | Calories from Fat 22

	% Daily Value*
Total Fat 2.4g	**4%**
Cholesterol 0mg	**0%**
Sodium 1mg	**0%**
Potassium 63mg	**2%**
Total Carbohydrates 1.8g	**1%**
Dietary Fiber 0.6g	**2%**
Sugars 1.2g	
Protein 0.3g	

Vitamin A 19%	•	Vitamin C 63%
Calcium 0%	•	Iron 1%

Nutrition Grade B+

* Based on a 2000 calorie diet

Nutritional Analysis

Good points

- No cholesterol
- Very low in sodium
- Very high in vitamin A
- High in vitamin B6
- Very high in vitamin C

Bad points

- High in sugar

Perfect Peppers on the Grill

Prep Time: 15 Minutes

Cook Time: 45 Minutes

Ready In: 1 Hour

Servings: 6

INGREDIENTS

2 tbsp. olive oil

50g pine nuts

140g long grain rice

2 garlic cloves, chopped

350g vegetable stock

1 bunch spring onions sliced thinly

140g cherry tomatoes, halved

150g ball mozzarella, chopped

140g gorgonzola

Handful each of parsley and basil, chopped

3 red and 3 yellow peppers

String, for tying

INSTRUCTIONS

1. Make the stuffing: heat up the oil in a medium pan with a lid and fry the pine nuts until slightly toasted, after that put in the rice and fry until the grains are glossy. Blend in the garlic, after that include the stock and bring to the boil. Cover up and cook for 10 minutes, until the rice is soft .Remove from the heat, cool down slightly and blend in the spring onions, cherry tomatoes, mozzarella, gorgonzola and fresh herbs. Season well and allow to cool.

2. Stuffing the peppers: trim around the stalk from one pepper, take off and put aside. Create one slit down the length of the pepper and open up gently. Take out the seeds and membrane.

3. Spoon some filling into the pepper cavity, taking care do not overfill.

4. Use approximately a meter length of kitchen string and wrap the center point several times around the pepper stalk, tying it firmly.

5. Top with the stalk and wrap the ends of the string several times around the pepper to secure the filling. Tie the ends in a knot .Repeat with the other peppers.

6. Grill the stuffed peppers over medium heat for 15-20 minutes, rotating carefully until the peppers are evenly browned. Don't worry too much whether the string chars in case the peppers split too much – wrap them in a sheet of foil and complete cooking in the aluminum foil wrappers.

Nutrition Facts

Serving Size 143 g

Amount Per Serving

Calories 271 | Calories from Fat 155

% Daily Value*

Total Fat 17.2g	**26%**
Saturated Fat 5.5g	**28%**
Cholesterol 22mg	**7%**
Sodium 323mg	**13%**
Potassium 136mg	**4%**
Total Carbohydrates 23.0g	**8%**
Dietary Fiber 1.9g	**8%**
Sugars 1.4g	
Protein 8.4g	

Vitamin A 10% • Vitamin C 6%

Calcium 12% • Iron 9%

Nutrition Grade C+

* Based on a 2000 calorie diet

Nutritional Analysis

Good points

- Low in sugar
- High in manganese

ɪtes

ɪtes

ɘs

4 aborigines, cut into 1cm slices lengthways

8 plum tomatoes, each cut into 3 thick slices

2 bunches of spring onions, trimmed

150ml extra-virgin olive oil

2 tbsp. white wine vinegar

3 plump garlic cloves, crushed

2 x 100g packs firm goat's cheese

Extra-virgin olive oil for drizzling

Large handful of fresh basil leaves

8 flour tortillas

INSTRUCTIONS

1. Place the sliced up aborigines, tomatoes and whole spring onions into a sizable shallow dish. Whisk the olive-oil, white wine vinegar and also garlic along with plenty of seasoning, pour over the vegetables and toss well.

2. Grill the aborigine slices right over a medium high heat for 4-5 minutes both sides, until tender and marked. Remove and place into a sizable shallow bowl. Barbecue the tomatoes and spring onions for 3-4 minutes, flipping once. Put into the aborigines. Crumble the goat's cheese over the hot vegetables and drizzle with extra virgin olive-oil. Toss very gently.

3. To serve up, scatter the basil leaves over the vegetables .Warm the floured tortillas on the barbecue for 1-2 minutes, flipping one time. Allow each guest grab a spoonful from the platter of vegetables and goat's cheese and fold up in a warm tortilla.

Nutrition Facts

Serving Size 170 g

Amount Per Serving

Calories 234   Calories from Fat 168

	% Daily Value*
Total Fat 18.7g	**29%**
Saturated Fat 2.7g	**13%**
Trans Fat 0.0g	
Cholesterol 0mg	**0%**
Sodium 27mg	**1%**
Potassium 298mg	**9%**
Total Carbohydrates 17.0g	**6%**
Dietary Fiber 2.9g	**11%**
Sugars 5.1g	
Protein 2.9g	

Vitamin A 16%	•	Vitamin C 48%
Calcium 4%	•	Iron 5%

Nutrition Grade B

* Based on a 2000 calorie diet

Nutritional Analysis

Good points

- No cholesterol
- Very low in sodium
- Very high in vitamin C

Stuffed Sweet Potatoes

Prep Time: 15 Minutes

Cook Time: 30 Minutes

Ready In: 45 Minutes

Servings: 8

INGREDIENTS

8 medium sweet potatoes

4 tsp olive oil

4 tbsp. Greek yogurt

1 spring onion, sliced

INSTRUCTIONS

1. Rub every potato with a bit of oil and salt, after that wrap in a double covering of aluminum foil.

2. The moment the barbecue coals are gleaming red, place the potatoes directly on them. Prepare for 15 mines, flip with tongs, and then cook for 15 mines more. Take off one, unwrap and check it is grilled through.

3. Peel back the top of the aluminum foil from every potato, split open and top with a spoonful of yogurt and a few spring onion slices.

Nutrition Facts

Serving Size 4 g

Amount Per Serving

Calories 21   Calories from Fat 21

% **Daily Value***

Total Fat 2.3g	**4%**
Cholesterol 0mg	**0%**
Sodium 0mg	**0%**
Potassium 5mg	**0%**
Total Carbohydrates 0.1g	**0%**
Protein 0.0g	

Vitamin A 0%	•	Vitamin C 1%
Calcium 0%	•	Iron 0%

Nutrition Grade D

* Based on a 2000 calorie diet

Nutritional Analysis

Good points

- No cholesterol
- Very low in sodium
- Very low in sugar

Lemon Zest Potato Salad

Prep Time: 20 Minutes

Cook Time: 20 Minutes

Ready In: 40 Minutes

Servings: 6

INGREDIENTS

900g halved new potatoes

3 tsp olive oil

Juice 1 lemon

1 tsp each toasted black mustard seeds and toasted cumin seeds

1 finely chopped green chili (optional)

½ finger-length piece grated ginger

Pinch turmeric

4 sliced spring onions

Chopped Salad INSTRUCTIONS

1.In a bowl , combine 5 coarsely grated carrots , 1 peeled , deseeded and finely chopped pepper , 2 finely chopped tomatoes , 1 finely chopped onion , ½ cucumber , cut into small portions , pinch golden caster sugar , 1 tsp cumin seeds and 3 tbsp. white wine vinegar . Season with salt. Preferred tossed at the very last minute.

INSTRUCTIONS

2. Boil the new potatoes for 15 mines until just moderately overcooked but keeping their form. While still warm, toss with all of the other INGREDIENTS. Season.

This can be created as much as a day in advance and chilled, but pull out of the refrigerator a good couple of hours before serving.

Nutrition Facts

Serving Size 13 g

Amount Per Serving

Calories 23   Calories from Fat 21

% Daily Value*

Total Fat 2.4g	**4%**
Cholesterol 0mg	**0%**
Sodium 2mg	**0%**
Potassium 29mg	**1%**
Total Carbohydrates 0.8g	**0%**
Protein 0.2g	

Vitamin A 2%	•	Vitamin C 3%
Calcium 1%	•	Iron 1%

Nutrition Grade B-

* Based on a 2000 calorie diet

Nutritional Analysis

Good points

- No cholesterol
- Very low in sodium
- High in vitamin C

Chapter 3

Barbecued Potato Wedges

Prep Time: 15 Minutes

Cook Time: 15 Minutes

Ready In: 30 Minutes

Servings: 8

INGREDIENTS

4 large potatoes, unpeeled

A little olive oil

Few fresh rosemary sprigs, leaves stripped

2 garlic cloves, very finely sliced (optional)

INSTRUCTIONS

1. Cut the potatoes to the thickness of your little finger, removing the rounded end pieces. Tip into a pan of cool salted water and bring to the boil. Simmer for 3 minutes until just cooked, and then drain. This task can be performed a day in advance.

2. Rub and massage each and every slice with just a little oil and barbecue until golden and charred on both sides. Put into a dish and sprinkle with rosemary and garlic, if using. Drizzle with some more olive-oil, season with salt and serve.

Nutrition Facts

Serving Size 185 g

Amount Per Serving

Calories 128   Calories from Fat 2

% **Daily Value***

Total Fat 0.2g	**0%**
Cholesterol 0mg	**0%**
Sodium 11mg	**0%**
Potassium 754mg	**22%**
Total Carbohydrates 29.2g	**10%**
Dietary Fiber 4.4g	**18%**
Sugars 2.1g	
Protein 3.1g	

Vitamin A 0%	•	Vitamin C 61%
Calcium 2%	•	Iron 5%

Nutrition Grade A

* Based on a 2000 calorie diet

Nutritional Analysis

Good points

- Very low in saturated fat
- No cholesterol
- Very low in sodium
- High in dietary fiber
- High in potassium
- High in vitamin B6
- Very high in vitamin C

Grilled Zucchini Sandwiches

Prep Time: 20 Minutes

Ready In: 20 Minutes

Servings: 1 Giant Sandwich

INGREDIENTS

1 medium zucchini, cut into 4 long planks

2 teaspoons olive oil

Kosher salt and freshly ground black pepper

Pinch of herbs de Provence

1/2 tablespoon unsalted butter, room temperature, plus more for spreading on the bread

1/2 tablespoon all-purpose flour

1/2 cup milk

1/2 tablespoon Dijon mustard

Pinch of freshly grated nutmeg

2 (2/3-inch) slices of fresh white sandwich bread

1 1/4 cups grated Emmenthaler cheese

INSTRUCTIONS

1. Pre-heat a grill or grill pan to high heat. Toss the zucchini slightly with olive-oil, salt, pepper, and herbs de Provence. Grill until charred and cooked through, for 4 minutes per side. Put aside.

2. In a compact saucepan, melt the butter. Whisk in the flour and cook over minimal heat for 1 minute. Whisk in the milk, and keep whisking until the mix has thickened enough to thickly coat a spoon. Put aside.

3. Pre-heat broiler to high. Spread one side of every piece of bread with butter. Place 6 tablespoons grated cheese on un-buttered side of one slice

of bread. Top with the zucchini, and then top with 6 more tablespoons cheese. Close sandwich, buttered side out. Toast the sandwich in a nonstick pan over moderate heat until golden brown on each side, for 3 minutes per side.

4. Position the sandwich on a foil-lined rimmed baking sheet. Spread the top with the white sauce, and then top with remaining 1/2 cup cheese. Broil until the cheese is toasted. Serve up immediately.

Nutrition Facts

Serving Size 347 g

Amount Per Serving

Calories 244 — Calories from Fat 166

% Daily Value*

Total Fat 18.4g	**28%**
Saturated Fat 6.6g	**33%**
Trans Fat 0.0g	
Cholesterol 25mg	**8%**
Sodium 207mg	**9%**
Potassium 601mg	**17%**
Total Carbohydrates 16.1g	**5%**
Dietary Fiber 2.6g	**10%**
Sugars 9.1g	
Protein 7.2g	

Vitamin A 12%	•	Vitamin C 56%
Calcium 18%	•	Iron 6%

Nutrition Grade B

* Based on a 2000 calorie diet

Nutritional Analysis

Good points

- Very high in vitamin B6
- Very high in vitamin C

Bad points

- High in saturated fat

Original Marinated Thai Tofu Skewers

Prep Time: 15 Minutes

Cook Time: 1 hour

Ready In: 1 Hour 15 Minutes

Servings: 4

INGREDIENTS

Marinade:

1/2 cup roughly chopped Thai basil

1/4 cup olive oil

1/4 cup fresh lime juice

1 tablespoon dark soy sauce

1 stalk lemongrass, cut into bits

2 garlic cloves, grated

2 inch knob ginger, grated

1 inch knob galangal, grated

1 Thai Chile pepper, minced

1 teaspoon palm sugar

Pepper

Salt

To serve:

2 zucchini, sliced horizontally in 1 inch chunks

8 lemongrass stalks

Shiitake or criminal mushrooms

2 lb. extra firm tofu, cut horizontally into 1 1/2 inch slabs

2 medium onions, cut into wedges

Olive oil

INSTRUCTIONS

1. Line a chopping board with a paper towel. Position the tofu slabs on the paper towel. Top with another paper towel and chopping board.

2. Place something heavy (such as canned goods or perhaps a cooking pot) atop the second chopping board. Allow to press for 15 minutes, after that slice each slab into 3 equal cubes.

3. Pressing the tofu , although it appears kind of excessive , helps to compact the tofu so that it does not fall apart on the skewer and enables more of the marinade to penetrate . Position cubes in a resalable bag together with the marinade INGREDIENTS. Refrigerate for a minimum of 1 hour, but up to 8.

4. For the meantime , take away the external leaves of the lemongrass to get to the harder "core" but if whole , cut off the top as well as the bottom 4 inches or so . Slice one end into a point. Thread the tofu along with the vegetables on the lemongrass.

5. Brush with olive-oil. Position on the hottest section of the grill and cook until heated through, making certain both sides cooks equally. The tofu and vegetables should caramelize. Serve up warm.

Nutrition Facts

Serving Size 395 g

Amount Per Serving

Calories 307   Calories from Fat 201

% Daily Value*

Total Fat 22.3g	**34%**
Saturated Fat 3.8g	**19%**
Cholesterol 0mg	**0%**
Sodium 78mg	**3%**
Potassium 679mg	**19%**
Total Carbohydrates 12.8g	**4%**
Dietary Fiber 4.3g	**17%**
Sugars 5.4g	
Protein 20.5g	

Vitamin A 4%	Vitamin C 36%
Calcium 49%	Iron 23%

Nutrition Grade A-

* Based on a 2000 calorie diet

Nutritional Analysis

Good points

- No cholesterol
- Low in sodium
- High in calcium
- High in manganese
- High in phosphorus
- High in selenium
- High in vitamin C

Chickpea English Muffin Burgers

Prep Time: 15 Minutes

Cook Time: 25 Minutes

Ready In: 40 Minutes

Servings: 4

INGREDIENTS

1 can (15 ounces) chickpeas, drained and rinsed

4 scallions, trimmed

2 slices white sandwich bread

1/3 cup peanuts or almonds, unsalted

1/2 teaspoon ground cumin

1 tablespoon fresh ginger, chopped

Coarse salt and ground pepper

1 large egg

Olive oil

1 tablespoon Dijon mustard

1/3 cup mayonnaise

Whole-wheat English muffins and lettuce, to serve with burgers

INSTRUCTIONS

1. Warm grill to high. In a food processor, mix chickpeas, scallions, bread, peanuts, cumin, and ginger; season with salt and pepper. Pulse until roughly chopped.

2. Take away half the mixture to a bowl; add egg to food processor. Process until smooth; add to reserved mixture in bowl, and blend well.

3. Make the mixture into four 3/4-inch-thick patties. Brush both sides gen~~~~~~~ ~~~~ ~~~ grill until charred, 3 to 5 minutes per side. Serve up the ~~~~~~~~~~~~ ns with lettuce, mustard, and mayonnaise.

tion Facts

g

rving

	Calories from Fat 127
	% Daily Value*
1g	**22%**
t 2.2g	**11%**
Trans Fat 0.0g	
Cholesterol 52mg	**17%**
Sodium 207mg	**9%**
Potassium 174mg	**5%**
Total Carbohydrates 9.1g	**3%**
Dietary Fiber 1.8g	**7%**
Sugars 2.3g	
Protein 5.5g	

Vitamin A 5%	•	Vitamin C 5%
Calcium 4%	•	Iron 8%

Nutrition Grade B
* Based on a 2000 calorie diet

Nutritional Analysis

Good points

- High in manganese

Avocado and Roasted Tomatoes

Prep Time: 15 Minutes

Cook Time: 15 Minutes

Ready In: 30 Minutes

Servings: 4

INGREDIENTS

3 avocados

3 limes, cut in wedges

1-1/2 cup grape tomatoes

1 cup corn, fresh or frozen

1 cup onion, chopped

3 serrano or jalapeno peppers

2 garlic cloves, peeled

1/4 cup cilantro leaves, chopped

1 tbsp. olive oil + more for avocados

Himalayan salt, to taste

Ground black pepper, to taste

Black beans (optional)

INSTRUCTIONS

1. Ready the grill for a medium-hot fire.

2. Place the oven to roast setting at 550ºF or as high as it can go.

3. Line a baking sheet with parchment paper. Combine tomatoes to a bowl along with the garlic cloves and corn. If utilizing fresh corn, cut it from the cob and add to a bowl. Chop onion and add to bowl. Take off stems, membranes, and seeds from 2 of the peppers. Dice and add to the

bowl. For even more heat, leave the seeds and membranes in the peppers. Place 1 tablespoon of olive-oil to the bowl, salt and pepper, then blend well to coat all the vegetables. Turn vegetables onto parchment paper.

4. Place into oven and roast until slightly browned, rotating 1 - 2 times during cooking. Meanwhile, slice the avocados in half lengthwise. Coat every half of the flesh side of the avocado, with a bit of olive-oil. Position the avocados, flesh side down on the grill and grill until warmed throughout and somewhat charred. If you don't wish to start the grill, roast the avocados in the oven with the other vegetables.

5. Flip grilled avocados over and fill up the middle with the roasted vegetable mix.

6. Top with chopped cilantro and chopped up peppers.

7. Squeeze with fresh lime juice and serve up with added wedges of lime juice on the side.

Nutrition Facts

Serving Size 244 g

Amount Per Serving

Calories 334   Calories from Fat 267

% Daily Value*

Total Fat 29.7g	**46%**
Saturated Fat 6.2g	**31%**
Trans Fat 0.0g	
Cholesterol 0mg	**0%**
Sodium 289mg	**12%**
Potassium 923mg	**26%**
Total Carbohydrates 18.7g	**6%**
Dietary Fiber 11.8g	**47%**
Sugars 3.5g	
Protein 3.8g	

Vitamin A 19%	•	Vitamin C 43%
Calcium 4%	•	Iron 8%

Nutrition Grade B

* Based on a 2000 calorie diet

Nutritional Analysis

Good points

- No cholesterol
- High in dietary fiber
- High in vitamin C

Chapter 4

Marvelous Pumpkin Burgers

Prep Time: 15 Minutes

Cook Time: 30 Minutes

Ready In: 45 Minutes

Servings: 4

INGREDIENTS

1 1/2 cup pumpkin flesh

1 medium-sized onion

3 – 4 mushrooms

1/2 bell-pepper

4 – 6 slices sun-dried tomatoes

1 – 2 tbsp. hemp seeds

2 tbsp. chickpea flour

1 tbsp. semolina (can be replaced with rice flour)

Vegetable oil for frying

Salt and pepper to taste

Optional

Dried herbs (thyme or marjoram)

INSTRUCTIONS

1. Shred the pumpkin utilizing a fine rasp. Set it in a deep bowl, put in salt and stir nicely. Put aside for a few minutes.

2. Slice the onion, bell-pepper and mushrooms and stir-fry all of them for a moment until tender. Then, mix them in a blender or a food processor until puree consistency.

3. Slice the sun-dried tomatoes.

4. Blend the grated pumpkin, vegetable puree and tomatoes all together.

5. Add the chickpea flour, semolina and hemp seeds and stir. Combine salt and pepper to taste and herbs (optional). Allow for the blend to cool down for 30 minutes in the refrigerator.

6. Heat the oil in a deep pan. Utilizing two tablespoons, form the burgers and bake them over medium heat on each side until golden brown.

Nutrition Facts

Serving Size 128 g

Amount Per Serving

Calories 62 | Calories from Fat 5

	% Daily Value*
Total Fat 0.5g	**1%**
Cholesterol 0mg	**0%**
Sodium 4mg	**0%**
Potassium 311mg	**9%**
Total Carbohydrates 12.8g	**4%**
Dietary Fiber 2.8g	**11%**
Sugars 2.8g	
Protein 2.5g	

Vitamin A 92%	•	Vitamin C 11%
Calcium 3%	•	Iron 6%

Nutrition Grade A

* Based on a 2000 calorie diet

Nutritional Analysis

Good points

- Very low in saturated fat
- No cholesterol
- Very low in sodium
- High in dietary fiber
- High in manganese
- High in potassium
- Very high in vitamin A
- High in vitamin C

Bad points

- High in sugar

Tomatoes Filled to Burst with Cannellini and Couscous

Prep Time: 12 Minutes

Cook Time: 48 Minutes

Ready In: 1 Hour 20 Minutes

Servings: 6

INGREDIENTS

1 box (6 ounces) roasted garlic with olive oil-couscous mix, divided

4 tablespoons olive oil (preferably extra-virgin), divided

1/2 cup prechopped onion, minced

6 large ripe but firm tomatoes (10 ounces each; about 4 3/4 pounds total)

1 can (15 ounces) cannellini beans, rinsed and drained

2 tablespoons chopped fresh parsley

1 1/2 teaspoons Italian seasoning

INSTRUCTIONS

1. Pre-heat the Barbecue grill. Coating a 9" x 6" disposable foil pan with cooking spray. Measure 1/2 cup of the couscous and 1 tablespoon of the flavoring packet from the mixture. Put aside. Keep the left over couscous and flavoring packet for another dish.

2. In a mid-size pan, heat 2 tablespoons of the oil over moderate heat. Put in the onion and cook for 3 minutes, or until the onion is softened. In the meantime, cut 1/4" slices from the tomato tops. Dispose of the tops. With a serrated knife or spoon, scoop out the tomato flesh, leaving 1/4"-thick walls. Put aside. Thinly chop the tomato flesh. Include in the onion along with the beans, parsley, Italian seasoning, pepper, and the set aside couscous and seasoning. Blend to mix. Spoon into the set aside tomato shells, mounding slightly. Spoon any additional stuffing into the bottom of the pan. Drizzle with the left over 2 tablespoons of oil. Cover up with aluminum foil.

3. Position on the grill off of direct heat. Grill, rotating the pan frequently, for approximately 45 minutes, or until the tomatoes are soft and the tops are golden. Leave to stand for 20 minutes

Nutrition Facts

Serving Size 13 g

Amount Per Serving

Calories 84   Calories from Fat 84

	% Daily Value*
Total Fat 9.7g	**15%**
Saturated Fat 1.4g	**7%**
Cholesterol 1mg	**0%**
Sodium 1mg	**0%**
Potassium 8mg	**0%**
Total Carbohydrates 0.2g	**0%**
Protein 0.0g	

Vitamin A 2%	•	Vitamin C 3%
Calcium 0%	•	Iron 1%

Nutrition Grade D

* Based on a 2000 calorie diet

Nutritional Analysis

Good points

- Very low in cholesterol
- Very low in sodium
- Very low in sugar

Barbecue Seitan Ribs

Prep Time: 15 Minutes

Cook Time: 1 hour 15 Minutes

Ready In: 1 Hour 30 Minutes

Servings: 6

INGREDIENTS

Spice Rub

1/4 cup raw turbinate sugar

2 Tbs. smoked paprika

1 tsp. cayenne pepper

3 garlic cloves, minced

2 tsp. dried oregano

1 Tbs. Kosher salt

1 ½ tsp. ground black pepper

¼ cup fresh parsley, minced

Balsamic BBQ Sauce

½ cup apple cider vinegar

¾ cup balsamic vinegar

¾ cup maple syrup

1 1/2 cups ketchup

1 red onion, minced

1 garlic clove, minced

1 serrano Chile, seeded and minced

For the Seitan Ribs

2 cups vital wheat gluten

3 Tbs. Mexican Chile powder

3 Tbs. dried onion powder

3 Tbs. dried garlic powder

¼ cup nutritional yeast

½ tsp. ground black pepper

2 cups water

¼ cup tahini

¼ cup low-sodium soy sauce

2 tsp. liquid smoke

INSTRUCTIONS

1. In a compact bowl, blend the INGREDIENTS for the spice rub. Blend well and put aside.

2. In a compact saucepan over moderate heat, mix the apple cider vinegar, balsamic vinegar, maple syrup, ketchup, red onion, garlic and Chile. Blend and let simmer, uncovered, for approximately 1 hour. Increase the heat to medium-high and cook for 15 more minutes until the sauce thickens. Stir it frequently. If it appears too thick, include some water.

3. Pre-heat the oven to 350 degrees. In a sizable bowl, mix the dry INGREDIENTS for the seitan and blend well. In smaller sized bowl, blend the wet INGREDIENTS. Put in the wet INGREDIENTS to the dry and combine until just combined. Knead the dough slightly until everything is combined and the dough starts to feel elastic.

4. Oil or spray a baking dish. Place the dough to the baking dish, flattening it and stretch it out to fit the dish. Cut the dough into 8 pieces then in half to make 16 thick ribs. (Note: if you would like the ribs thinner, this really is plenty of dough to fill up 2 baking sheets. If you really want them thick, it will be enough for just one).

5. Top the dough with the spice rub and massage it in a little. Bake the seitan for 40 to 60 minutes or until the seitan possesses a firm consistency to it (leaner ribs is going to cook quicker). Take out the dish from the oven. Recut the pieces and very carefully remove all of them from the baking tray.

6. Raise the oven temperature to 400 degrees. Smooth the ribs with Barbecue sauce and put them on a baking sheet. Place the ribs back into the oven for just 10 minutes so the sauce gets a little charred. On the other hand, you may cook the sauce-covered ribs on a Barbecue grill or in a grill skillet.

Tempeh Ribs

1. Cut a package of tempeh into 6 or 8 rectangles, based how wide you would like the "ribs" to be. If you would like them to be leaner, slice the tempeh in half like a bagel first. I prefer my tempeh slim as a result I actually do this added slice all of the time. Steam the tempeh for 15 minutes until it softens a little.

2. Coat the tempeh with the spice rub. Prepare the tempeh ribs in the oven or in a pan until browned on each side. This will take about 8 minutes per side. Brush the Barbecue sauce on the tempeh and cook for an additional couple of minutes until mildly charred.

Nutrition Facts

Serving Size 295 g

Amount Per Serving

Calories 306   Calories from Fat 59

% **Daily Value***

Total Fat 6.6g	**10%**
Saturated Fat 0.9g	**5%**
Trans Fat 0.0g	
Cholesterol 0mg	**0%**
Sodium 2448mg	**102%**
Potassium 753mg	**22%**
Total Carbohydrates 58.4g	**19%**
Dietary Fiber 5.3g	**21%**
Sugars 41.4g	
Protein 8.5g	

Vitamin A 43%	•	Vitamin C 30%
Calcium 13%	•	Iron 25%

Nutrition Grade A

* Based on a 2000 calorie diet

Nutritional Analysis

Good points

- Low in saturated fat
- No cholesterol
- Very high in manganese
- High in vitamin A

Bad points

- Very high in sodium
- Very high in sugar

Gluten-Free Zesty Italian Vegan Sausages

Prep Time: 15 Minutes

Cook Time: 20 Minutes

Ready In: 35 Minutes

Servings: 4

Create spice mix ahead of time. Put aside.

Spice Mix

1 tsp. garlic powder

1 ½ tsp. fennel, crushed

½ tsp. black pepper

½ tsp. salt

1 tsp. sweet paprika

1 tsp. smoked paprika

¼ – ½ tsp. red pepper flakes

½ tsp. oregano

1/8 tsp. allspice

2 tsp. + 2 tsp. olive oil

¾ cup mushrooms, chopped

¼ cup onion, finely chopped

1 garlic clove, minced

2 cups or 1-15 oz. can of pinto beans, drained and rinsed

1 Tbs. sun-dried tomato paste

¼ cup nutritional yeast

½ cup brown rice flour

1 tsp. xanthan gum

1 Tbs. gluten-free tamari

1 Tbs. balsamic vinegar

(2 Tbs. of gluten-free, vegan Worcestershire Sauce can be used in place of the tamari and vinegar)

A few drops of Liquid Smoke (optional)

INSTRUCTIONS

1. Heat up a skillet with 2 tsp. of olive-oil. Sauté the onions, mushrooms and garlic until softened. Put aside and allow to cool. In a sizable bowl, insert the pinto beans and mash them up. You can utilize a fork, a potato masher or your hands. I choose to use my hands. If you wish to use a food processor, apply a rough chop. You don't want a puree.

2. After that include the tomato paste, nutritional yeast, and brown rice flour. Blend well. Sprinkle the xanthan gum over the mixture and combine it well.

3. Insert the cooled vegetable mix to the bowl and blend it into the dry INGREDIENTS. Put in the tamari and balsamic vinegar to the bowl and combine all of it up nicely. If you utilize the Liquid Smoke, put it in now too.

4. Separate the mixture into 4 parts. Form each part into a log. Wrap the logs separately in aluminum foil and steam all of them for 15-20 minutes. After that refrigerate for a couple hours or overnight, when possible. This helps them firm up even more.

5. Whenever ready to use, unwrap and cook them however you choose. You can serve them with sautéed bell peppers and onions

Nutrition Facts

Serving Size 64 g

Amount Per Serving

Calories 125   Calories from Fat 12

% Daily Value*

Total Fat 1.4g	**2%**
Trans Fat 0.0g	
Cholesterol 0mg	**0%**
Sodium 305mg	**13%**
Potassium 438mg	**13%**
Total Carbohydrates 23.3g	**8%**
Dietary Fiber 4.5g	**18%**
Sugars 1.5g	
Protein 7.1g	

Vitamin A 13%	*	Vitamin C 5%
Calcium 2%	*	Iron 19%

Nutrition Grade A

* Based on a 2000 calorie diet

Nutritional Analysis

Good points

- Low in saturated fat
- No cholesterol
- High in dietary fiber
- High in iron
- Very high in manganese
- Very high in niacin
- High in pantothenic acid
- High in phosphorus
- Very high in riboflavin
- Very high in thiamin
- Very high in vitamin B6

Chilled Carrot Slaw Dish

Prep Time: 12 Minutes

Ready In: 12 Minutes

Servings: 4

INGREDIENTS

2 pounds carrots, approximately 12 to 15 medium

1/2 cup mayonnaise

Pinch salt

1/3 cup sugar

1/2 cup canned, crushed pineapple, drained thoroughly of all liquid

1/2 cup raisins

2 teaspoons curry powder

1 teaspoon minced garlic

Pinch celery seed and/or caraway seed, optional

INSTRUCTIONS

1. Cleanse the carrots and peel, if needed. Utilizing a vegetable peeler, cut the carrots into wide noodle-shaped strips.

2. In a sizable mixing bowl whisk jointly the mayonnaise , salt , sugar , pineapple , raisins , curry powder , garlic , and celery seed and/or caraway seed , if utilizing . Put in the carrots and toss to mix.

3. Serve up immediately or refrigerate for 1 hour to serve cold.

Nutrition Facts

Serving Size 325 g

Amount Per Serving

Calories 354   Calories from Fat 91

% Daily Value*

Total Fat 10.1g	**16%**
Saturated Fat 1.5g	**8%**
Trans Fat 0.0g	
Cholesterol 9mg	**3%**
Sodium 443mg	**18%**
Potassium 988mg	**28%**
Total Carbohydrates 64.8g	**22%**
Dietary Fiber 6.6g	**26%**
Sugars 44.1g	
Protein 5.3g	

Vitamin A 762%   •   Vitamin C 24%
Calcium 19%   •   Iron 8%

Nutrition Grade B+

* Based on a 2000 calorie diet

Nutritional Analysis

Good points

- Low in saturated fat
- Low in cholesterol
- Very high in vitamin A

Bad points

- Very high in sugar

Chapter 5

Sweet Teriyaki Marinade Shish Kabobs

Prep Time: 3 Hours

Cook Time: 15 Minutes

Ready In: 3 Hours 15 minutes

Servings: 6

INGREDIENTS

Sweet teriyaki marinade and sauce

1 cup soy sauce

½ cup vegetable oil

1/4 cup pineapple juice + 1/2 cup pineapple juice, divided

3 tablespoons brown sugar

2 tablespoons dry sherry

4 medium cloves garlic, minced (about 1 tablespoon)

2 tablespoons minced fresh ginger root (about one thumb-sized hunk)

1/2 teaspoon dry mustard

1 tablespoon cornstarch

2 tablespoons water

Shish kabobs

1/2 pound white button mushrooms, wiped clean with a damp paper towel

1 small green bell pepper

1 small red bell pepper

1 cup fresh pineapple chunks (about half a small pineapple)

1 medium sweet onion, cut into large wedges (cut in half, then quarters, then eighths)

Cooked white rice to serve alongside, if desired

Optional addition for vegetarian shish kabobs

1 Field Roast "sausage" link (You can use smoked apple sage for this recipe), cut into 1-inch slices

Add for meat-eaters

1/2 pound petite sirloin, cut into 1-inch square chunks

1 sausage of your choice pineapple bacon chicken sausage), cut into 1-inch slices

Equipment

12 12-inch wood/bamboo skewers

Outdoor bob or grill pan

INSTRUCTIONS

1. Position cut-up steak in a quart-size or larger zipper bag. Add 1/2 cup of marinade over the steak and seal up well, swishing the meat and marinade to help assure even coverage . Place into the refrigerator for at minimum 2 hours (up to 12 hours).

2. Set aside 1 cup of marinade for basting at a later date. Refrigerate in a protected container.

3. Set the left over marinade in a compact saucepan. Include 1/2 cup pineapple juice and heat over mid-size heat, uncovered, stirring frequently to avoid scorching. Blend cornstarch and water together in a little bowl. When the marinade comes to a boil, whisk in cornstarch and water, stirring consistently until sauce thickens. Take away from heat and allow to cool, and then refrigerate in a sealed container until ready to serve.

4. Soak the skewers. Fill up a long baking dish about 1/3 full with water and set skewers in the water. Enable to soak for a minimum of a half hour. This will help prevent the skewers from burning up once on the grill.

5. If serving with rice, you want to begin it now.

6. Put together the shish kabobs. Carefully thread vegetables, pineapple, and Field Roast or meat onto skewers in whichever order you prefer. I prefer to utilize bell peppers on the ends simply because they help to keep everything on.

7. Heat up your grill to about 350 - 375 degrees (moderate heat). Set shish kabobs on grill. Baste with the 1 cup reserved teriyaki marinade (segregating portions for meat/non-meat kabobs if desired). Cook, rotating frequently to help ensure even cooking and continuing to baste occasionally, for approximately 15 minutes until vegetables are tender and meat is cooked throughout.

8. Serve up with rice (if preferred) and teriyaki sauce for dipping/drizzling as desired.

Nutrition Facts

Serving Size 182 g

Amount Per Serving

Calories 245   Calories from Fat 167

	% Daily Value*
Total Fat 18.5g	**29%**
Saturated Fat 3.6g	**18%**
Trans Fat 0.0g	
Cholesterol 0mg	**0%**
Sodium 2402mg	**100%**
Potassium 334mg	**10%**
Total Carbohydrates 17.2g	**6%**
Dietary Fiber 2.1g	**8%**
Sugars 10.3g	
Protein 4.5g	

Vitamin A 16%	•	Vitamin C 79%
Calcium 2%	•	Iron 12%

Nutrition Grade B-

* Based on a 2000 calorie diet

Nutritional Analysis

Good points

- No cholesterol
- High in manganese
- Very high in vitamin B6
- Very high in vitamin C

Bad points

- Very high in sodium
- High in sugar

Broccoli and Mozzarella Cheese Pizza

Prep Time: 15 Minutes

Cook Time: 15 Minutes

Ready In: 30 Minutes

Servings: 2

INGREDIENTS

1 package Flat-out Thin Crust Flatbreads

1 (8-ounce) container ricotta cheese

2 garlic cloves, minced

1/2 teaspoon salt

1/4 teaspoon pepper

1/2 teaspoon red pepper flakes

2 cups shredded mozzarella cheese

1/4 cup shredded Parmesan cheese

1 head broccoli, cut into small pieces

INSTRUCTIONS

1. In a bowl, combine ricotta, garlic, salt, pepper, and red pepper flakes. Scatter about 1/4 cup of the ricotta mix evenly on the crust. Sprinkle with mozzarella cheese. Be generous.

2. Add in broccoli pieces. Grill over low heat. Cover up and cook until the crust crisps up so the cheese melts. Let sit for one minute before cutting. Or else the cheese will drip everywhere. I prefer to sprinkle with red pepper flakes and slice.

Nutrition Facts

Serving Size 231 g

Amount Per Serving

Calories 483   Calories from Fat 262

% **Daily Value***

Total Fat 29.1g	**45%**
Saturated Fat 17.6g	**88%**
Trans Fat 0.0g	
Cholesterol 95mg	**32%**
Sodium 1404mg	**58%**
Potassium 166mg	**5%**
Total Carbohydrates 11.2g	**4%**
Protein 45.2g	

Vitamin A 28%	•	Vitamin C 2%
Calcium 112%	•	Iron 4%

Nutrition Grade D+

* Based on a 2000 calorie diet

Nutritional Analysis

Good points

- Very low in sugar
- Very high in calcium
- High in phosphorus
- High in selenium

Bad points

- High in saturated fat
- High in sodium

Barbecue Deviled Eggs

Prep Time: 10 Minutes

Cook Time: 20 Minutes

Ready In: 30 Minutes

Servings: 24

INGREDIENTS

12 eggs

3 tablespoons mayonnaise

2 tablespoons neely's barbecue sauce

1 tablespoon yellow mustard

1 teaspoon yellow mustard

1 pinch kosher salt

Fresh ground black pepper

Hot sauce (a dash or two will do)

2 scallions, thinly sliced

Smoked paprika (or regular paprika, to garnish)

INSTRUCTIONS

1. Bring a mid-size pan of water to a boil, and then turn down to a simmer.

2. Utilizing a slotted spoon, gradually lower eggs into water and simmer for 9 minutes. Decrease temperature if it simmers too much, you do not want the eggs to break.

3. Drain out water from the saucepan and run cool water over the eggs until they are cool enough to handle.

4. Peel the eggs and slice in half.

5. Take out yolks and place in a bowl.

6. Add the mayonnaise, neely's barbecue sauce, mustard, salt, pepper, and hot sauce to taste; whisk until smooth.

7. Use a spoon to scoop the yolk mixture into the whites. (If you desire, you may use a pastry bag to pipe the yolk mix into whites).

8. Garnish the tops with lightly sliced scallions and a sprinkle of paprika.

Nutrition Facts

Serving Size 26 g

Amount Per Serving

Calories 40　　　　　　　Calories from Fat 26

% Daily Value*

Total Fat 2.8g	**4%**
Saturated Fat 0.8g	**4%**
Trans Fat 0.0g	
Cholesterol 82mg	**27%**
Sodium 62mg	**3%**
Potassium 34mg	**1%**
Total Carbohydrates 0.7g	**0%**
Protein 2.8g	

Vitamin A 2%	•	Vitamin C 0%
Calcium 1%	•	Iron 2%

Nutrition Grade B-

* Based on a 2000 calorie diet

Nutritional Analysis

Good points

- Low in sugar
- High in phosphorus
- High in riboflavin
- Very high in selenium
- High in vitamin B12

Bad points

- Very high in cholesterol

Grilled Cottage Cheese Filled Mushrooms

Prep Time: 2 Minutes

Cook Time: 30 Minutes

Ready In: 32 Minutes

Servings: 1

INGREDIENTS

2 medium mushrooms (your favorite variety)

1/4 teaspoon black pepper, ground

4 tablespoons cottage cheese

INSTRUCTIONS

1. Take away stalks from mushrooms and stuff with cottage cheese until level with the top and sprinkle a small amount of ground pepper over the top.

2. Cook on an oiled Barbecue plate with hood down but off of direct heat - so well to the side of a burner which is turned on. Choose the coolest spot in your BBQ.

3. In around 20-30 minutes make sure you notice the top of the mushrooms turning soft and dark in color, they are ready to serve at that moment.

Nutrition Facts

Serving Size 93 g

Amount Per Serving

Calories 60   Calories from Fat 11

% Daily Value*

Total Fat 1.2g	**2%**
Saturated Fat 0.7g	**4%**
Cholesterol 5mg	**2%**
Sodium 232mg	**10%**
Potassium 175mg	**5%**
Total Carbohydrates 3.6g	**1%**
Dietary Fiber 0.5g	**2%**
Sugars 0.8g	
Protein 8.9g	

Vitamin A 1%	•	Vitamin C 2%
Calcium 4%	•	Iron 7%

Nutrition Grade A

* Based on a 2000 calorie diet

Nutritional Analysis

Good points

- High in iron
- High in niacin
- High in pantothenic acid
- High in phosphorus
- High in riboflavin
- Very high in selenium
- Very high in vitamin B6
- High in vitamin B12

Bad points

- High in sodium

Barbecued Tofu with Sauce

Prep Time: 10 Minutes

Cook Time: 1 Hour

Ready In: 1 Hour 10 Minutes

Servings: 3

INGREDIENTS

1 (14 ounce) packages extra firm tofu

1 medium onion, chopped

4 garlic cloves, minced

1/2 cup ketchup

1 tablespoon whole grain mustard

1 tablespoon turbinate sugar (or other sugar or agave nectar)

2 tablespoons chipotle chills in adobo, chopped

1 teaspoon tamari soy sauce

1 tablespoon cider vinegar

1/4 teaspoon cinnamon

1/4 teaspoon fresh ground black pepper

1/4 teaspoon celery seed (optional)

INSTRUCTIONS

1. Chop each block of tofu into 9 slices. Position them on a double layer of paper towels or a clean tea towel (non-fuzzy) and place another double layer over them. Press firmly with your hands to take away as much moisture as possible. Allow them to sit on the absorbent material while you make the sauce.

2. Heat a saucepan and include the onion. Cook, stirring, over medium-high heat until onion starts to brown, a minimum of 6 minutes. Insert the

garlic and cook for an additional minute. Put in all left over INGREDIENTS (except for the tofu) and cook, stirring, over moderate to low heat, for approximately 15-20 minutes, until thick and fragrant.

3. Pre-heat oven to 425°F Position a silicone baking mat on a cookie sheet or oil a long, rectangular baking dish. Brush one side of each and every slice of tofu with a lean layer of sauce and put it on the pan sauce-side down. Spread left over sauce on the tops and edges of the tofu. Bake for about 25-30 minutes, until tofu is firm and just starting to brown at the edges. Serve hot.

Nutrition Facts

Serving Size 226 g

Amount Per Serving

Calories 159   Calories from Fat 53

% **Daily Value***

Total Fat 5.9g	**9%**
Saturated Fat 1.2g	**6%**
Trans Fat 0.0g	
Cholesterol 0mg	**0%**
Sodium 598mg	**25%**
Potassium 432mg	**12%**
Total Carbohydrates 17.9g	**6%**
Dietary Fiber 2.4g	**9%**
Sugars 11.5g	
Protein 12.5g	

Vitamin A 8%	•	Vitamin C 17%
Calcium 30%	•	Iron 15%

Nutrition Grade A

* Based on a 2000 calorie diet

Nutritional Analysis

Good points

- No cholesterol
- High in calcium
- Very high in manganese
- High in phosphorus
- High in selenium
- High in vitamin C

Bad points

- High in sodium
- High in sugar

Chapter 6

Mediterranean Grilled Vegetable Blend

Prep Time: 25 Minutes

Cook Time: 10 Minutes

Ready In: 35 Minutes

Servings: 9

INGREDIENTS

3 large Portobello mushrooms, sliced

1 each medium sweet red, orange and yellow peppers. Sliced

1 medium zucchini, sliced

10 fresh asparagus spears, cut into 2-inch lengths

1 small onion, sliced and separated into rings

3/4 cup grape tomatoes

1/2 cup fresh sugar snap peas

1/2 cup fresh broccoli florets

1/2 cup pitted Greek olives

1 bottle (14 ounces) Greek vinaigrette

1/2 cup crumbled feta cheese

INSTRUCTIONS

1. In a sizable resealable plastic bag, blend the mushrooms, peppers and zucchini. Include the asparagus, onion, tomatoes, peas, broccoli and

olives. Add vinaigrette into bag; seal bag and turn to coat. Refrigerate for a minimum of 30 minutes.

2. Dispose of marinade. Transfer vegetables to a grill wok or basket. Grill, uncovered, over mid-size heat for 8-12 minutes or until soft, stirring frequently. Position on a serving dish; sprinkle with cheese.

Nutrition Facts

Serving Size 88 g

Amount Per Serving

Calories 40   Calories from Fat 17

% **Daily Value***

Total Fat 1.9g	**3%**
Saturated Fat 1.3g	**6%**
Trans Fat 0.0g	
Cholesterol 7mg	**2%**
Sodium 99mg	**4%**
Potassium 186mg	**5%**
Total Carbohydrates 4.0g	**1%**
Dietary Fiber 1.4g	**5%**
Sugars 2.2g	
Protein 2.5g	

Vitamin A 10%	•	Vitamin C 24%
Calcium 6%	•	Iron 5%

Nutrition Grade A

* Based on a 2000 calorie diet

Nutritional Analysis

Good points

- High in calcium
- High in dietary fiber
- High in iron
- High in manganese
- High in phosphorus
- High in potassium
- High in riboflavin
- High in thiamin
- Very high in vitamin A
- High in vitamin B6
- Very high in vitamin C

Bad points

- High in saturated fat
- High in sodium
- High in sugar

Pineapples on the Grill

Prep Time: 15 Minutes

Ready In: 15 Minutes

Servings: 2

INGREDIENTS

1 medium fresh pineapple

3 tablespoons agave nectar

2 tablespoons lime or lemon juice

1/4 teaspoon cinnamon

INSTRUCTIONS

1. Trim down the leafy crown from the pineapple and throw away. Position the pineapple firmly up-right, cut off the tough skin, using downward motions with a sharpened knife. Slice the pineapple flesh off of the tough core, and then cut into 1/2-inch-thick chunks, a little bit bigger than bite-sized. Grilled pineapple recipe in a sizable mixing bowl, toss the pineapple with agave nectar and lime juice. Spread in the cinnamon and toss again. Prepare the grill. Set the pineapple portions on the grill in one layer. Grill for 3 to 4 minutes on both sides, just until you obtain some nice grill marks. Don't over-cook, as the pineapple could possibly dry out.

Nutrition Facts

Serving Size 0 g

Amount Per Serving

Calories 1   Calories from Fat 0

% **Daily Value***

Total Fat 0.0g	**0%**
Trans Fat 0.0g	
Cholesterol 0mg	**0%**
Sodium 0mg	**0%**
Potassium 1mg	**0%**
Total Carbohydrates 0.2g	**0%**
Protein 0.0g	

Vitamin A 0%	•	Vitamin C 0%
Calcium 0%	•	Iron 0%

Nutrition Grade A-

* Based on a 2000 calorie diet

Nutritional Analysis

Good points

- No saturated fat
- No cholesterol
- Very low in sodium
- Very high in calcium
- Very high in dietary fiber
- High in iron
- Very high in manganese

Grilled Peppered Pizza

Prep Time: 15 Minutes

Cook Time: 30 Minutes

Ready In: 45 Minutes

Servings: 4

INGREDIENTS

1 pound prepared pizza dough, preferably whole-wheat

1/2 cup prepared pesto

4 ripe plum tomatoes, thinly sliced

1/2 cup crumbled feta cheese

Freshly ground pepper, to taste

1/4 cup lightly packed fresh basil leaves, torn

INSTRUCTIONS

1. Heat grill to medium-high.

2. In the meantime, position dough on a slightly floured surface area. Separate into 4 pieces. Roll each piece into an 8-inch round crust, approximately 1/4 inch thick. Set crusts on a floured baking sheet. Take crusts and toppings out to the grill.

3. Place crusts on grill (they won't remain completely rounded). Cover up grill and cook until crusts are slightly puffed and undersides are lightly browned, about 3 minutes.

4. Using tongs, turn over crusts. Promptly spread pesto over crusts. Top with tomatoes. Sprinkle with feta and pepper. Cover up grill and cook until the undersides are slightly browned, about 3 minutes more. Sprinkle with basil and serve at once.

ition Facts

2 g

rving

	Calories from Fat 38
	% Daily Value*
g	7%
2.8g	14%
7mg	6%
g	9%
Potassium 263mg	8%
Total Carbohydrates 7.1g	2%
Dietary Fiber 1.4g	5%
Sugars 5.7g	
Protein 4.1g	

Vitamin A 17%	•	Vitamin C 48%
Calcium 11%	•	Iron 4%

Nutrition Grade A

* Based on a 2000 calorie diet

Nutritional Analysis

Good points

- High in calcium
- High in pantothenic acid
- High in phosphorus
- High in riboflavin
- Very high in vitamin A
- High in vitamin B6
- Very high in vitamin C

Bad points

- High in saturated fat
- High in sodium
- High in sugar

Grilled Tofu with Yogurt Sauce

Prep Time: 15 Minutes

Cook Tim(

Ready In:

Servings:

INGREDI

2 teaspc

1 teasp(

1/2 teaspoon ground cumin

1/2 teaspoon ground coriander

1/4 teaspoon ground turmeric

3 tablespoons extra-virgin olive oil

1 tablespoon minced garlic

1 tablespoon lime juice

2 14-ounce packages extra-firm or firm water-packed tofu, drained

2/3 cup nonfat plain yogurt

6 tablespoons sliced scallions or chopped fresh cilantro for garnish

INSTRUCTIONS

1. Preheat grill to medium-high.

2. Combine paprika, 1/2 teaspoon salt, cumin, coriander and turmeric in a small bowl. Heat oil in a small skillet over medium heat. Add garlic, lime juice and the spice mixture; cook, stirring, until sizzling and fragrant, about 1 minute. Remove from the heat.

3. Slice each tofu block crosswise into 6 slices; pat dry. Use about 3 tablespoons of the spiced oil to brush both sides of the tofu slices;

sprinkle with the remaining 1/2 teaspoon salt. (Reserve the remaining spiced oil.)

4. Oil the grill rack. Grill the tofu until it has grill marks and is heated through, 2 to 3 minutes per side.

5. Combine yogurt with the reserved spiced oil in a small bowl. Serve the grilled tofu with the yogurt sauce, garnished with scallions (or cilantro), if desired.

Nutrition Facts

Serving Size 39 g

Amount Per Serving

Calories 85   Calories from Fat 67

% **Daily Value***

Total Fat 7.5g	**12%**
Saturated Fat 1.3g	**6%**
Cholesterol 2mg	**1%**
Sodium 408mg	**17%**
Potassium 97mg	**3%**
Total Carbohydrates 3.0g	**1%**
Sugars 2.0g	
Protein 1.8g	

Vitamin A 9%	•	Vitamin C 2%
Calcium 6%	•	Iron 2%

Nutrition Grade B-

* Based on a 2000 calorie diet

Nutritional Analysis

Good points

- Very low in cholesterol
- High in vitamin A

Bad points

- High in sodium

Vegan Chicken, Agave Nectar with Chipotle Sauce

Prep Time: 10 Minutes

Cook Time: 10 Minutes

Ready In: 20 Minutes

Servings: 4

INGREDIENTS

1/4 cup fresh lime juice

2 Tbsp. Just-Like-Honey or agave nectar

4 cloves garlic, peeled and chopped

1 serrano Chile or jalapeno pepper, minced

1 chipotle Chile, in adobo

Pepper, to taste

1/4 tsp. cornstarch

1 Tbsp. cilantro, minced

1 lb. mock chicken or seitan

INSTRUCTIONS

1. Preheat the grill.

2. In a food processor or blender, puree lime juice, "honey," garlic, serrano Chile or jalapeno pepper, chipotle chili, pepper, and cornstarch.

3. Transfer the mixture to a medium-sized sauce pan and boil until slightly thickened, about 1 minute. Stir in the cilantro.

 Brush the "chicken" lightly with the glaze.

4. Grill for 3 to 4 minutes on each side, turning once. Just before removing the "chicken" from the grill, baste with the remaining glaze.

5. Remove from the grill and serve.

Nutrition Facts

Serving Size 32 g

Amount Per Serving

Calories 35   Calories from Fat 3

% Daily Value*

Total Fat 0.4g	**1%**
Cholesterol 0mg	**0%**
Sodium 113mg	**5%**
Potassium 21mg	**1%**
Total Carbohydrates 1.4g	**0%**
Protein 5.6g	

Vitamin A 1%	Vitamin C 4%
Calcium 1%	Iron 0%

Nutrition Grade B

* Based on a 2000 calorie diet

Nutritional Analysis

Good points

- Low in saturated fat
- No cholesterol
- Low in sugar
- High in vitamin C

Bad points

- High in sodium

Delightfully Grilled Lasagna with Vegetables

Prep Time: 15 Minutes

Cook Time: 1 Hour

Ready In: 1 Hour 15 Minutes

Servings: 10

INGREDIENTS

3 eggplants, cut lengthwise into 1/4-inch slices (about 3 pounds)

3 zucchini, cut lengthwise into 1/8-inch slices (about 1 1/4 pounds)

Cooking spray

1 teaspoon salt, divided

3/4 teaspoon freshly ground black pepper, divided

2 red bell peppers, quartered and seeded

1 (15-ounce) container fat-free ricotta cheese

1 large egg

3/4 cup grated Asia go cheese, divided

1/4 cup minced fresh basil

1/4 cup minced fresh parsley

9 lasagna noodles, divided

1 (26-ounce) jar tomato-basil spaghetti sauce (such as Muir Glen), divided

3/4 cup (3 ounces) shredded part-skim mozzarella cheese, divided

1/4 cup commercial pesto (such as Alissa)

INSTRUCTIONS

1. Pre-heat grill.

2. Coat eggplants and zucchini with cooking spray. Spread with 1/2 teaspoon salt and 1/4 teaspoon black pepper. Grill eggplant and zucchini 1 1/2 minutes on both sides or basically until soft. Cool; blend in a large bowl.

3. Position bell peppers on grill, skin-side down; grill 3 minutes or until tender. Slice into (1-inch-wide) strips. Include bell peppers to eggplant mix.

4. Blend ricotta cheese, egg, 1/2 cup Asia go cheese, basil, parsley, left over 1/2 teaspoon salt, and remaining 1/2 teaspoon black pepper.

5. Prepare the lasagna noodles based on package INSTRUCTIONS, omitting the salt and the fat.

6. Pre-heat oven to 375°.

7. Spread 1/2 cup spaghetti sauce in base of a 13 x 9-inch cooking dish coated with cooking spray. Organize 3 noodles over tomato sauce. Top with half of eggplant mix. Spread half of ricotta cheese mix over eggplant mix; sprinkle with 1/4 cup mozzarella cheese.

8. Organize 3 noodles and 1 cup of spaghetti sauce over cheese; cover up with the remaining eggplant mix. Top with left over ricotta mixture. Spread pesto over ricotta; scatter with 1/4 cup mozzarella cheese. Cover up with remaining 3 noodles.

9. Spoon 1 cup spaghetti sauce over noodles. Dab with remaining 1/4 cup Asia go cheese and remaining 1/4 cup mozzarella cheese.

10. Bake at 375° for 1 hour. Let stand 15 minutes before serving.

Nutrition Facts

Serving Size 306 g

Amount Per Serving

Calories 149   Calories from Fat 53

% Daily Value*

Total Fat 5.9g	**9%**
Saturated Fat 3.2g	**16%**
Trans Fat 0.0g	
Cholesterol 36mg	**12%**
Sodium 355mg	**15%**
Potassium 653mg	**19%**
Total Carbohydrates 15.8g	**5%**
Dietary Fiber 7.0g	**28%**
Sugars 7.1g	
Protein 10.5g	

Vitamin A 25%	•	Vitamin C 77%
Calcium 21%	•	Iron 6%

Nutrition Grade A

* Based on a 2000 calorie diet

Nutritional Analysis

Good points

- High in calcium
- High in dietary fiber
- High in manganese
- High in phosphorus
- High in potassium
- High in selenium
- High in vitamin A
- High in vitamin B6
- Very high in vitamin C

Bad points

- High in saturated fat
- High in sugar

Reddish-Bean Burgers with Avocado and Lime Wedges

Prep Time: 30 Minutes

Cook Time: 40 Minutes

Ready In: 1 Hour

Servings: 4

INGREDIENTS

2 cans (15.5 ounces each) red kidney beans, rinsed and drained

1 medium carrot, peeled and shredded (about 1/2 cup)

1 teaspoon chili powder

1 teaspoon dried oregano

3/4 cup dried breadcrumbs

2 large eggs, lightly beaten

Coarse salt and freshly ground pepper

3 tablespoons extra-virgin olive oil

Hamburger buns, romaine-lettuce leaves, sliced avocado, sliced red onion, sour cream, and lime wedges, for serving

INSTRUCTIONS

1. Slightly mash beans in a sizable bowl, leaving some whole. Include carrot, chili powder, oregano, breadcrumbs, and eggs. Season generously with salt and pepper; mix until completely combined. Separate mixture into 4 portions and shape into patties.

2. Heat 2 tablespoons oil in a large nonstick pan over moderate heat. Put in patties and cook, undisturbed, until base forms a browned crust and the majority of oil is absorbed, 10 to 12 minutes. Turn patties and include remaining 1 tablespoon oil to pan, swirling to coat bottom.

3. Cook, undisturbed, until browned on other side and heated throughout, 8 to 10 minutes. Serve up on buns with accompaniments.

Nutrition Facts

Serving Size 73 g

Amount Per Serving

Calories 215   Calories from Fat 128

% **Daily Value***

Total Fat 14.2g	**22%**
Saturated Fat 2.5g	**13%**
Trans Fat 0.0g	
Cholesterol 93mg	**31%**
Sodium 200mg	**8%**
Potassium 141mg	**4%**
Total Carbohydrates 16.9g	**6%**
Dietary Fiber 1.7g	**7%**
Sugars 2.3g	
Protein 6.1g	

Vitamin A 58%   •   Vitamin C 3%

Calcium 6%   •   Iron 10%

Nutrition Grade B+

* Based on a 2000 calorie diet

Nutritional Analysis

Good points

- Very high in vitamin A

Bad points

- High in cholesterol

Conclusion

First and foremost I would like to thank you for your purchase and for using this book for your vegetarian cookout needs. I hope that you have enjoyed these delicious and delectable vegetarian grilling recipes. If you are looking for more amazingly simple vegetarian recipes please check out my other books on kindle.

-Diana Welkins

Vegetarian Freezer Meal Recipes: Time Saving Vegetarian Freezer Meal Recipes

Vegetarian Lifestyle Cookbook: 20 Delightful Vegetarian Lasagna Recipes

30994119R00055

Printed in Great Britain
by Amazon